WAR IN THE HEAVENS

VICTOR ANSOR

WAR IN THE HEAVENS

An Exposition into Strategic Spiritual Warfare

CHALFANT ECKERT
PUBLISHING

War In The Heavens

Copyright © 2015 Victor Ansor. All Rights Reserved.

No rights claimed for public domain material, all rights reserved. No parts of this publication may be reproduced, stored in any retrieval system, or transmitted in any form or by any means, electronic, mechanical, recording, or otherwise, without the prior written permission of the author. Violations may be subject to civil or criminal penalties.

Library of Congress Control Number: 2015943866

ISBN: 978-1-63308-149-9 (paperback)
ISBN: 978-1-63308-150-5 (ebook)

Interior Design by R'tor John D. Maghuyop
Cover Illustration by Miša Jovanović

CHALFANT ECKERT
PUBLISHING

1028 S Bishop Avenue, Dept. 178
Rolla, MO 65401

Printed in the United States of America

To my mother Agatha, who took me to church and pointed me to Jesus.

To all born again Christians who are enforcing the kingdom of God on the earth through strategic spiritual warfare.

Life is warfare, and not a playfare.
—Bishop David Oyedepo

THE MANDATE

Unto me, who am less than the least of all saints, is this grace given, that I should preach among the Gentiles the unsearchable riches of Christ; And to make all men see what is the fellowship of the mystery, which from the beginning of the world had been hid in God, who created all things by Jesus Christ: To the intent that now unto the principalities and powers in heavenly places might be known by the church the manifold wisdom of God, According to the eternal purpose which he purposed in Christ Jesus our Lord
Ephesians 3:8-11

TABLE OF CONTENTS

Introduction		11
Definition of Terms		15
Chapter 1:	Why the Fight?	17
Chapter 2:	Know Your Enemy	23
Chapter 3:	Prerequisites For Strategic Spiritual Warfare	27
Chapter 4:	How To Fight	37
Chapter 5:	The Weapons of Warfare	45
Chapter 6:	The Battle Ground	59
Chapter 7:	Spiritual Allies	67
Chapter 8:	An Enemy Has Done This	71
Chapter 9:	Why You Must Not Lose the Fight	83
Chapter 10:	Strategic Spiritual Warfare	87
Chapter 11:	Victory	105

INTRODUCTION

Many Christians today do not know about spiritual warfare. Most are content with just living a normal, natural life with very little thought to what is happening around them in the realm of the spirit. They are satisfied with accepting life at face value, without the additional responsibilities that may accompany increased knowledge of spiritual warfare.

A lot of Christians just desire to live a normal life, without being conscious of the fact that from the moment they give their lives to Jesus, the battle lines are drawn and there is a war. Whether they are interested or not, the battle is targeted at them, and very often there are casualties. If we should liken spiritual war to a natural war, there are many on the battlefield who are not really interested in fighting in battle. They are not equipped and not prepared to combat the enemy, so even without their knowledge, they suffer defeat.

You can be born again and still experience failure in every aspect your life. This is not normal, for there is nothing normal on this earth. The physical world is ruled by the spiritual world. In essence, what can be seen and that which appeals to our five physical senses is really just a shadow of the real world. In fact, the Scripture confirms this in John 3:27:

> *...a man can receive nothing, except*
> *it be given him from heaven.*

No man (meaning in the flesh in the physical world) can receive anything, except it is given to him from above (from the spiritual world). So before you can receive or experience anything on this earth, it must come from the unseen world. For example, delay in marriage is a spiritual attack launched against your marital destiny from the kingdom of darkness. If you consistently fail in examinations, you are under spiritual attack. If your husband or wife suddenly begins to misbehave and you become frustrated and move out or plan to, this is a spiritual battle against your family launched by the enemy from the spiritual world.

You don't have to cry because when you do, you have lost the battle in that area and your enemies, who are demons working through human agents, will celebrate their victory over you. What you must do is to buck up and fight. The weakness of a lot of churches is failing to make the connection between what we are experiencing in the physical world and the spiritual connotations attached to it. The reality is that what is spiritual will manifest itself in the natural world. When we fail to connect the spiritual aspect of our earthly experiences, we employ natural means to combat our problems, and we meet with very little success. You cannot fight a spiritual war with natural weapons.

WAR IN THE HEAVENS

There is a serious war going on every day in the spiritual world that I will refer to as the *heavenlies*. The heavenlies are classified into levels. The first heaven is the firmament from Genesis 1, which includes the fowls of the air and Earth's atmosphere. Satan exercises his power in this arena because God cast him out of heaven and Satan now rules over "all kingdoms of the inhabited earth" (Luke 4:5-6). The second heaven is outer space, where the sun, moon, and stars are in the orbit God set them in, and the third heaven is where God dwells and is the highest level. This is where God and His holy angels live. The spiritual world is superior to the physical world, and everything happening in the physical has its real origins in the spiritual world.

The kingdom of darkness, an invisible realm, is where evil is perpetrated in the highest order. In this kingdom, there exists cruelty and competition. This is where all the affliction of men and every form of wickedness emanates from. We see this in the following Scriptures:

> *...for the dark places of the earth are*
> *full of the habitations of cruelty.*
> Psalm 74:20

> *And we know that we are of God, and*
> *the whole world lies in wickedness.*
> 1 John 5:19

It is my understanding that not everyone we see or relate with are normal human beings. Someone may appear ordinary, but at night he or she may be in the spirit world as a witch or satanic agent. I once told someone that she needed to learn how to pray warfare prayer. She told me that there was no need for her to pray such prayers because she had not offended anyone. What she failed to understand was that from the moment she gave her life to Jesus, Satan declared her a person of interest, and demons were dispatched to bring her down. When you are not born again, the devil has no business to attend to with you because you already belong to him. But when you walk away from him at salvation, you become engaged in spiritual warfare and the only way out is to fight because he wants you back.

I strongly believe that this book will be an eye opener and will help to equip you to stand against the kingdom of darkness that is against you.

> *The thief cometh not, but for to steal,*
> *and to kill, and to destroy:*
> *I am come that they might have life, and*
> *that they might have it more abundantly.*
> John 10:10

DEFINITION OF TERMS

To understand the topic, we must first define the terms.

Strategic: Of or relating to the general plan that is created to achieve a goal in war, etc. (strategic. 2011. In *Merriam-Webster.com*)

Warfare: the waging of war against an enemy. Military struggle between two groups. (warfare. 2015. In *thefreedictionary.com*)

From the above definitions, we can say that strategic spiritual warfare is a plan to wage war against spiritual forces.

Before we can engage in strategic spiritual warfare, there must first be a plan.

Or what king, going to make war against another king, sitteth not down first and consulteth whether he be able with ten thousand to meet him that cometh against him with twenty thousand? Or else, while the other is yet a great way off, he sendeth an ambassage, and desireth conditions of peace.
Luke 14:31-32

In spiritual warfare, there must be casualties. Your enemies are not mere humans. You can't just arbitrarily decide one day to engage in spiritual warfare unprepared. The knowledge you acquire in this book will make you ready for war.

CHAPTER 1

WHY THE FIGHT?

There is a war going on in the heavenlies, whether we are willing to face it or not. Your reluctance to face the reality that there is a real battle going on does not negate its existence. It actually leaves you very vulnerable and depleted.

I want to look at the cause of the war and why we are involved.

ANGER

The Bible opens our understanding to the fact that the devil is bitter against man, and he has sworn to destroy man for no just cause.

> *Therefore rejoice ye heavens and ye that dwell in them. Woe to the inhabiters of the earth and of the sea! For the devil is come down unto you, having great wrath, because he knoweth that he hath but a short time.*
> Revelation 12:12

When the devil and his demons lost the war in heaven, he was thrown out, and he came down to the earth with great anger against God, and His greatest creation, man. The above Scripture says he came down with **great wrath,** the devil is not happy with man and he never will be.

GOD'S LOVE FOR MAN

God is in love with man. God loves man so much that it makes the devil envious. It was King David in Psalm 8:4 who asked this question that we see repeated in Hebrew 2:6:

> *What is man, that thou art mindful of him?*
> *Or the Son of man that thou visitest him?*

The devil is envious of man. He knows that man is ultimately the crown of God's creation, and he knows that God will do anything for man. This is confirmed in John 3:16 because God sent His only Son to die for man. This love has sparked so much hatred in Satan that he has vowed to destroy man by every possible means. So we can see that the battle started from the beginning, and we have a real enemy who will do all in his power to destroy us. The best and only real option is to fight back.

DOMINION

The conflict between good and evil is rooted in control. When God created man, He gave him control and dominion over everything on the earth.

> *And God blessed them and God said unto them*
> *be fruitful and multiply and replenish the earth,*
> *and subdue it: and have dominion over the fish*
> *of the sea and over the fowl of the air and over*
> *every living thing that move upon the earth.*
> Genesis 1:28

The authority God gave to man angered the devil because maybe he feels that too much has been given. He attempts to come in subtle ways to strip man of his authority. The devil wanted to have what man was given. It is the very reason he tried to overthrow God and failed miserably. He did not succeed, and he decided to get what he wanted through someone God gave dominion to. It appeared that he was succeeding until Jesus made an appearance and restored all that was lost when Adam fell into sin.

> *And Jesus came and spake unto them, saying,*
> *All power is given unto me in*
> *heaven and in earth.*
> Matthew 28:18

Satan has no power or dominion over man. Jesus stripped him of his power. Man no longer has an excuse to hang around the devil. Adam lost dominion when he sinned, but Jesus restored it in Himself and has passed it back to mankind. The devil hates Jesus, and he hates men. He attempts to utterly destroy men, who were created in the image and likeness of God. When Jesus came and paid the price to redeem mankind from the devil, his hatred for man increased. When you walk out on the devil by giving your life to Jesus, he forms weapons against you in an attempt to bring you down.

WORSHIP

Spiritual conflicts are sometimes centered in worship. God is the absolute authority and He alone is to be worshiped. The devil craves worship and that is why he wants to be exalted to the position of God so that he can receive worship.

> *I will ascend above the heights of the clouds; I will be like the most high.*
> Isaiah 14:14

The battle for the soul of man is about worship. God's purpose for creating man was to worship Him. Jesus says in Matthew 4:10:

WAR IN THE HEAVENS

*Then saith Jesus unto him, Get thee hence, Satan: for it is written, Thou shall **worship** the Lord thy God, and him only shall thou serve.*

We can see from the above text that even when the devil confronted Jesus, he demanded worship. The devil wants worship because this has been his desire from the beginning. The forces of good and evil are fighting for humanity's worship. You must be prepared. Otherwise, you will be crushed. The devil is bent on destroying his opponent or anyone who refuses to give him what he wants. You must be conscious and be equipped to confront him.

CHAPTER 2

KNOW YOUR ENEMY

It is one thing to know that we are caught in a war, and another thing to know who your enemy is. The devil is a ruthless field marshal. He has been fighting since before you were even born. In fact, he fought in heaven, in the presence of God and His holy angels. He is not a cheap enemy but an experienced fighter.

Know that your adversary the devil is like a roaring lion seeking whom he may devour.
1 Peter 5:8

The knowledge of your enemy and his devices will help you to prepare for battle. Before any nation goes to war, (true even in ancient times of warfare), it is mandatory to find out all they can about the enemy. Spies are often sent to observe the opponent, find out what weapons they are using, the size of the army and the nature of the commander. This information helps in knowing how to approach the enemy. The knowledge of who your enemy is will be vital to your winning the war.

Know that the devil is not your friend, he hates you and wants to destroy you completely. You must know who your enemy is, and be ready to fight. Your enemy, the devil and his host of demons, don't sleep. They are always planning how to destroy your life, marriage, family, business, and career. The knowledge of these foes will help you to be on your feet and be ready to face them.

THE HANDS OF ESAU

We know the story of Esau and Jacob, how Jacob went in and deceived his father Isaac and received the blessing that was meant for Esau.

> *And Jacob went near unto Isaac his father,*
> *and he felt him and said, the voice is Jacob's*
> *voice, but the hands are the hands of Esau.*
> Genesis 27:22

Now, it was Jacob that was speaking, but the hand that caused the blessing to be given was that of Esau.

Every negative manifestation in the physical realm by humans is usually influenced by the devil. A man, woman, or child under attack is just a medium through which the devil manifest himself. The devil is very subtle. The Bible refers to him as a serpent.

> *Now the serpent was more subtle than any beast*
> *of the field which the Lord God has made. And*
> *he said unto the woman, yea hath God said,*
> *ye shall not eat of every tree of the garden?*
> Genesis 3:1

The devil will never appear before you physically and declare himself as the devil. If that were to occur, you might run. He often comes through human beings. He can come through your husband by influencing him to misbehave. Your husband is not the real enemy. If you can't look beyond what is physical to see your true enemy, you may lose your husband and, therefore, lose the war. The devil can attack you through your children by making them disrespect you or become very stubborn. He can also come through your church member, co-workers or your in-laws. The devil is the hand of Esau in every negative situation. With this knowledge, you will be able to identify the source of the conflict.

In any adverse situation, never see the physical person as the cause. There is another influencing that person to behave the way they do. There is a saying that "When you see a bird dancing on the road, know that the drummer is in the bush close by."

Allow me to share my story. I was a cultist. I was initiated into a most dangerous cult when I was in university. I also masturbated for twenty years every day. I was a drunkard and a chronic womanizer. I was such a very bad boy that my family wrote me off. They thought nothing good would have ever come out of me.

I delved into the occultic world in search of knowledge and wealth. You could not judge my heart by how I looked. I looked very innocent and naïve, but I was perpetrating evil. I was not the person doing all those evil things, but dark spiritual forces were working through me to destroy me. The devil was the enemy and I was his human puppet through which he manifested. Then the light of the glorious gospel of Jesus shined on me. I was delivered, and no longer a puppet in the hands of the devil.

The devil is the enemy and you must learn to identify him, or you will be walking in error and defeat. When there is fire, the source of the fire must be identified to effectively put out the fire. Otherwise, it will keep burning. May the Lord give you understanding.

CHAPTER 3

PREREQUISITES FOR STRATEGIC SPIRITUAL WARFARE

Before you engage in strategic spiritual warfare, you must know the prerequisites for engaging in such a war. Remember you are fighting against an experienced enemy. Some things must be in place.

1. You Must Be Born Again

If you are not born again, you cannot engage in spiritual warfare. Jesus said in Mark 3:24-26:

> *And if a kingdom be divided against itself, that kingdom cannot stand. And if a house be divided against itself, that house cannot stand. And if Satan rise up against himself, and be divided, he cannot stand, but hath an end.*

If you are not born again, you cannot fight the devil because you belong to him. You must first come out of his camp before you can stand against him. Have you ever seen a soldier turn against his army while he is still a part of that army? He must first desert his post, then he can join forces with another to fight. Jesus said in John 3:3 and 3:6:

> *Verily, verily I say unto thee, Except a man be born again, he cannot see the kingdom of God. ... That which is born of the flesh is flesh; and that which is born of the Spirit is spirit.*

If you are not born again, you are still in the flesh and you certainly cannot be in the flesh and fight spirits.

The Scripture says that if you are not born again, you cannot see the kingdom of God. You must first identify with God before you are able to engage in spiritual warfare. You need to accept Jesus Christ into your heart and life so you can be enlisted in the army that will enable you stand against your enemy the devil.

If you are not born again, and you want to be, please say this prayer before you continue:

> *Lord Jesus, I come to you. I know I am a sinner, and I believe you came and died for me that I might be saved. I accept you Jesus as my Lord and Saviour. Thank you, Jesus,*

*for forgiving me. Thank you for saving me.
Now I know my sins are forgiven. I am saved.
I am born again. I am a child of God, old
things are passed away and behold all things
are become new. In Jesus name, Amen.*

Now that you are born again, welcome into God's army. Jesus is the captain. You have been enlisted now on the winning side, therefore, equip yourself, for victory is already yours.

2. Be Full of the Word

Before engaging in strategic spiritual warfare, you must be full of the Word. In this kind of war, you do not go in empty handed. Your weapon is The Word.

> *The entrance of your word gives light; it
> giveth understanding unto the simple.*
> Psalm119:130

> *And the light shineth in darkness; and
> the darkness comprehended it not.*
> John 1:5

The enemy operates in darkness, so you need light to win. It is said that a wordless Christian is a powerless Christian. Learn to study the Word of God daily. Learn to memorize a verse of Scripture every day. These are the ammunition you are accumulating every day against the day of battle. Do not wait until a situation arises before you rush to the Bible and start opening frantically searching for a word to use.

An in-depth study of the Word will build what I call *The Word Bank* in you, and at every instance of attack from your enemy, you are already prepared to fire back.

In spiritual warfare, words matter. The Word you know is the victory you will have.

> *For I will give you a mouth and a*
> *wisdom, which all your adversaries shall*
> *not be able to gainsay nor resist.*
> Luke 21:15

The enemy cannot counter or resist the words you speak when he confronts you. Everything in the spiritual is about words. Before a Juju priest makes charm, he says some incantations, and the words he speaks during the incantation are what gives potency to the charm.

In spiritual warfare words matter. You must know what to say or else you will be defeated, and you can only know what to say by engaging in word study. Witches and warlocks use words to cripple and oppress their victims. What we call spiritual arrows are words released by wicked forces to whomever they target, and you can only reverse the arrows by a word. So it is word-for-word battle, and when the higher word is released, every other word becomes ineffective.

Most Christians see the Bible as a book they take to church only on Sundays. The Bible is not just another book, but a spiritual manual that demonstrates how we are to live on the earth. Study the Bible every day and it will prepare you for the battle ahead.

3. Purity

There is something I found out in the course of my quest into the kingdom of darkness. I found that those who want to advance to the highest rank in the kingdom of darkness always keep themselves pure. They avoid anything that will defile them. If they can do that in the kingdom of darkness, how about the kingdom of light? You cannot walk out of the bed of fornication and begin to fight against the powers of darkness. The devil will ask, "Who are you?" Demons asked some people who were trying to cast them out the following question found in Act 19:15:

> *And the evil spirit answered and said, Jesus I know, and Paul I know; but who are ye?*

You can only confront the devil when you are walking in purity. Make sure your hands are clean, and keep away from all filthiness. It is not only fornication and adultery that defiles.

There are many things people overlook, but these are the things that defile daily and rob us of legal standing against the devil. Do you know that something as simple as not paying the correct bus fare when you have money with you is a sin and it defiles? If you don't have money and need to be somewhere important, God will give you favour and the driver will accept whatever you have if you ask. But if you enter a bus and refuse to pay the correct fare, that is bad. If the driver or conductor forgets to collect money from you, don't keep it, pay him, and exercise integrity. You must be pure inside out. Do not take what does not belong to you thinking that no one sees you. God is seeing you.

Little lies you tell defile you. There is no little white lie. A lie is a lie no matter how you say it and who you say it to. Don't promise your child or children what you cannot do, and if you make a promise, do your best to keep it.

Don't defraud the government, but file correct tax.

Gossiping in church or in your workplace is a sin.

Buying something on credit just because your neighbor has it and you want it is also a sin.

Check yourself to see if you have done anything that would defile your body. Do away with it and you will be able to stand against the enemy.

If you dress in a way that you know will cause someone to look at you lustfully, then you need to desist from it. Trust your conscience to always tell you what is right and appropriate. If your conscience is not saying anything, you may have a dead conscience. Go to Jesus again. Avoid every appearance of evil.

In spiritual warfare, purity matters. Be at peace with everyone, hold no grudge and don't be bitter against anyone, for this is a strong spiritual blockade. The enemy you are about to fight knows your spiritual level, so you must check yourself. Conduct a personal spiritual diagnoses or self-examination.

4. Be Spiritual

The Bible says in 1 Corinthians 2:14:

> *But the natural man receiveth not the things of the Spirit of God: for they are foolishness unto him: neither can he know them, because they are spiritually discerned.*

A carnal man is a natural man. You can be saved yet you operate or live like the natural man. If you are not spiritual, you will not be sensitive to the things of the spirit.

One day as I was praying in tongues, immediately I saw myself in my younger brother's kitchen, still praying in tongues. I became conscious again and wondered what was wrong with my brother. I became worried and continued to think about the meaning of what was revealed to me. While still praying for him, two days later, I called to tell him I was praying for him. He began to thank God for using me to deliver him from a calamity. He said that two days earlier, something happened in his house but the next day God overturned it to his favour. If I were not praying in the Spirit, maybe something terrible would have happened.

Every child of God must be spiritual to effectively engage in spiritual warfare. Being spiritual helps us to sense any incursion from the pit of hell against our destiny. It also helps us get signals from heaven to help us fight against the power of darkness.

5. Be Baptized in The Holy Ghost

Holy Spirit baptism is vital in strategic spiritual warfare. When you are baptised in the Holy Ghost, you will speak in tongues (God-given prayer language) as evidence of that baptism.

The Scripture says in Roman 8:26:

> *Likewise the Spirit also helpeth our infirmities: for we know not what we should pray for as we ought: but the Spirit itself maketh intercession for us with groaning which cannot be uttered.*

Many times we don't know what to pray. When we pray in our known language, we quickly run out of words and become stranded at the altar of prayer. This becomes very dangerous as the opponent does not lack an arsenal and never rests in hurling attack after attack, so we need the Holy Spirit.

When we pray in tongues, the devil gets confused. Praying in tongues helps us to know what to do in the face of opposition. You cannot go far spiritually as a Christian if you are not baptised in the Holy Spirit.

CHAPTER 4

HOW TO FIGHT

There are many ways to fight this battle. The strategy you use in warfare depends largely on the type of enemy you are facing and the type of war that is at hand. In our context of spiritual warfare, we will be looking at ways in which you can fight your enemy.

Keep in mind that you cannot go to the war front casually, you must be strong and prepared for battle. The Scripture has given us a picture of how to be ready in Ephesians 6:10-18:

Finally, my brethren, be strong in the Lord and in the power of his might. Put on the whole armour of God, that ye may be able to stand against the wiles of the devil. For we wrestle not against flesh and blood, but against principalities, against powers, against the rulers of the darkness of this world, against spiritual wickedness in high places. Wherefore take unto you the whole armour of God, that ye may be able to withstand in the evil day, and having done all, to stand. Stand therefore, having your loins girt about with truth, and having on the breastplate of righteousness; And your feet shod with the preparation of the gospel of peace; Above all, taking the shield of faith, wherewith ye shall be able to quench all the fiery darts of the wicked. And take the helmet of salvation, and the sword of the spirit, which is the Word of God. Praying always with all prayer and supplication in the spirit, and watching thereunto with all perseverance and supplication for all saints;

Ephesian 6:10-18 is the blueprint for strategic spiritual warfare. It is a comprehensive plan on how to fight this battle.

The most important preparation you can make to fight a spiritual battle is to:

1. Put On The Whole Armour

You cannot just walk casually to the front of the war unprepared. If you do, you will become a casualty. Before you engage in a war, you must be properly dressed for it. No soldier wakes up in his pajamas and goes to war. Likewise, a soldier for Christ cannot enter the battle inappropriately dressed. Unfortunately, there are many lazy Christians who take life for granted, who expect God to do everything for them.

If you are born again, that is not a ticket for laziness. It is a call to warfare. The day you gave your life to Christ is the day you were conscripted into the army of Jesus and that army has no reserve, everyone is active. So you must put on the whole armour and prepare for war.

The enemies you are fighting against are:

a. Principalities
b. Powers
c. Rulers of darkness
d. Spiritual wickedness in high places

These are experienced spiritual entities that have no pity. They are ruthless and full of hate and you must be well equipped to challenge and overcome them. How?

1. Make sure your belt is tied around your waist with the truth of the gospel.
2. Your chest, which is your heart, is in right standing with God.
3. And above all take the shield of faith that will quench all the arrows the enemy will be throwing at you.

Faith is the only thing that can quench all the fiery darts of the devil and that is why he attempts to disqualify your faith. The devil will seek to destroy you by first attacking your faith. You need to ensure that your faith is in place and you will win the battle.

2. By Prayer

> *In everything by prayer and supplication,*
> *make your request known to God.*
> Philippians 4:6

It takes humility to pray and this warfare is fought with prayer. If you can humble yourself to get on your knees before God in prayer, you will be able to solicit help from the armies of heaven to your advantage. Ezra Taft Bensons says that "he who kneels before God can stand before anyone." This is true because if you can humble yourself to kneel before the almighty God and acknowledge Him as the one to whom the victory belongs, then you can stand before any devil. The Scripture says in 2 Chronicle 7:14:

> *If my people, which are called by my name,*
> *shall humble themselves, and pray, and seek*
> *my face and turn from their wicked ways;*
> *then will I hear from heaven, and will*
> *forgive their sin, and will heal their land.*

There is a famous saying I believe to be true, that half the battle is won when you go on your knees. If you are not humble, you won't pray. If you don't pray, you have lost the battle and the enemy will capture you as a prisoner of war and make you his houseboy, causing you to experience all kinds of afflictions. That is why you can go to church, but still nothing seems to work in your favour. You may listen to others testify, and wonder when will you be able to give your own testimony.

In praying, I recommend that you either fall to your knees or you stand on your feet. This shows readiness for warfare. Life is warfare, not fanfare. You can't be lying on your comfortable bed or couch and command authority in spiritual warfare. You must stand on your feet as this signals combat readiness, and shows that you are fit and capable. You don't sit down to confront an opponent. After doing all that is necessary, rise to your feet and begin to fight or counterattack as the case may be.

3. Maximizing the Night Hour

The midnight (Bible calls it the third watch of the night) is known to be the highest spiritual hour. This falls between the hours of 12 midnight to 3 a.m. The night season determines everything that happens during the day. It is at midnight that witches fly out for meetings and operations and return back at 4 a.m. Occultic powers begin their operations at midnight and so do Juju priests. Even armed robbers, especially in regions where they are prevalent, start operations at midnight. Midnight is a very significant time in spiritual warfare. It is the time you can stand to confront or counterattack the camp of your enemy.

The Bible says in Matthew 13:25:

But while men slept, his enemy came and sowed tares among the wheat, and went his way.

You can't be sleeping carelessly at night and expect to win in this war. While spiritual forces are up at night, you too must be up to battle with them, and by the morning, your victory is sure. If you sleep, the enemy will come and sow tares. Rise up, take your weapon and fight.

I am not saying you should not be sleeping at night, but if you notice something is wrong in your health, business, family, or academic life, don't keep quiet and sleep. When you notice any inconvenience in your life, know that it is an attack from hell, and you must fight back to regain all that was stolen from you.

I have seen a lot of strange things when I stand up to pray at midnight. I was in the habit of waking up at midnight to go to an incomplete church building and pray. I was living with an evangelist and a pastor. Whenever I stood up to go and pray, the evangelist and pastor were usually on the phone or sleeping. They always look at me as though I am stressing myself, and at that time I did not know that what I was doing had spiritual relevance and implication. Now I know I was doing a good thing because I am benefiting from it.

I always wake up at midnight and at 5 a.m. and declare into the heavenlies and command the ordinances of heaven to work for me. I sowed seeds into the ears of the moon, stars, the wind, and even the sun before it rose to shine, and amazing things began to happen in my life. That is why I am not surprised about the favour I am enjoying today. By the help of the Holy Spirit, I unknowingly commanded them to happen.

Most nights, I would go out to pray only in tongues, and sing praises. The Holy Ghost taught me to do those things, and I didn't even know I was fighting spiritual warfare. Now those night prayers are being manifested and it can do the same for you if you take the responsibility of engaging nighttime prayers. Don't wait until something happens. You can just take one or two nights a week and engage in prayers to aid you in strategic warfare. If you don't know what to pray, begin to pray in tongues and sing warfare songs like:

> *"Jehovah is your name*
> *Jehovah is your name*
> *Mighty warrior*
> *Great in battle*
> *Jehovah is your name"*

This is a powerful spiritual warfare song. With this song, you are invoking God to rise and fight for you. I have seen demons cast out by just singing the song. I have seen people vomiting witchcraft by singing the song. Great things can happen when you pray at night.

CHAPTER 5

THE WEAPONS OF WARFARE

In every battle, there are weapons to be used.

The Scripture in 2 Corinthians 10:4 says:

> *For the weapons of our warfare are not carnal, but mighty through God to the pulling down of strong holds; Casting down imaginations, and every high thing that exalts itself against the knowledge of God, and bringing into captivity every thought to the obedience of Christ; And having in a readiness to revenge all disobedience, when your obedience is fulfilled.*

From the above Scripture, we see that the weapons of this warfare are not carnal weapons. They are not guns, bullets, or anything natural. The text refers to them as mighty weapons through God. These weapons are able to pull down strongholds, cast down imaginations and can bring into captivity every thought to the obedience of Christ. I don't think any physical weapon exists that can battle spiritual forces. Let us look at these spiritual weapons which we can use in strategic spiritual warfare.

THE WORD OF GOD

Referring to the Bible as a spiritual weapon does not imply that we should put it under our pillow and sleep on it. The devil will still knock your head, even if you put the biggest Bible in the world under it. Many people keep the Bible by their bedside. In fact, I have known people who open Psalm 91 before they go to sleep. Some have a particular or special Bible they put in their car for protection. That does stop the devil from afflicting them. Some are even pressed by witches and wizards at night. It is not the physical Bible that is your weapon; it is the Word inside the Bible which you know.

I discovered in the Bible two Scriptures which I use in fighting spiritual battles, and these Scriptures help me issue specific commands:

> *Blotting out the handwriting of ordinances that was against us, which was contrary to us, and took it out of the way, nailing it to his cross*
> Colossians 2:14

You Can Command: Every handwriting of ordinance written against me, I blot it out by the blood of Jesus.

> *No weapon formed against thee shall prosper, and every tongue rising against thee in judgment thou shall condemn.*
> Isaiah 54:17

You Can Command: Any tongue that rise against me in judgment, I condemn them in Jesus name.

It is the knowledge of these Scriptures that help me issue commands in warfare. If I had put the Bible under my pillow without knowing what is written inside, I would have lost many great battles.

The Bible says in Colossians 3:16:

> *Let the Word of Christ dwell in you richly in all wisdom...*

You must be full of the Word of God to engage in spiritual warfare. When you study the Bible, the Word that you take in will be deposited inside you and when a situation arises, the Holy Spirit will teach you to use it. You can't give what you don't have.

If you face a situation, and suddenly a Scripture flows through your mind, it means you have read it. Even though you may not even know at the moment where in the Bible it may be, it was deposited inside you in the course of study. Some people will say, "I don't know where that Scripture came from." It came from where it was deposited and the Holy Spirit will bring Scriptures to our remembrance when we need them. The Word of God is your ammunition and your mouth is the gun.

THE NAME OF JESUS

The Scripture says in Proverbs 18:10:

> *The name of the LORD is a strong tower,*
> *the righteous run to it and are safe.*

And in Philippians 2:9

> *Therefore, God hath highly exalted him,*
> *and given him the name which is above*
> *every name that at the mention of the name*
> *of Jesus every knee must bow, of things*
> *in heaven, and things on the earth…*

When you call on the name of Jesus, all things are possible. Jesus is the highest name that Satan himself bows to when it is mentioned. When Jesus was resurrected, he told his disciples in Matthew 28:18:

> *…all power is given unto me*
> *in heaven and in earth.*

The name of Jesus commands authority and is a powerful spiritual weapon. There is no situation you face that will not bow at the mention of the name Jesus. There are diverse testimonies from people who used that name when confronted with spiritual attacks, and they were delivered. The dead can be raised at the mention of the name Jesus. I read a story of Bishop David Oyedepo, who was confronted with an accident. He shouted the name Jesus and he escaped.

The name of Jesus is not a punctuation mark as some people think, but it is a weapon. Your prayer is pointless without the name: Jesus.

The Bible says in Act 4:12:

> *Neither is there salvation in any other: for there is none other name under heaven given among men, whereby we must be saved.*

The name of Jesus is a vital weapon in fighting spiritual warfare.

THE BLOOD OF JESUS

In Revelation 12:11 the Bible says:

> *And they overcame him by the blood of the Lamb, and by the word of their testimony; and they loved not their life unto the death.*

The enemy you are fighting is not physical but spiritual and he is a Field Marshall in spiritual warfare. Therefore, one of your greatest weapons of attack against this foe is the blood of Jesus. You can overcome the devil quickly by using the blood of Jesus. When you are engaging in spiritual warfare, invoke the blood of Jesus. This is the greatest means to overcome the adversary.

I was sent to a branch of a company I used to work for. There were three of us in the vehicle. I was writing something in my diary when suddenly the steering of the pickup truck turned by itself and locked. The truck was heading to the forest on the interstate highway. I sat down quietly at the back watching the driver struggling to turn the steering and trying to apply the brake, but nothing worked.

My colleague, who was sleeping in the front, suddenly woke up and started screaming. He began to struggle with the driver and the steering wheel. Meanwhile, the truck has gone deep into the forest.

Suddenly, something began to stir inside me and I heard myself shout "the blood of Jesus." The truck stopped instantly. I experienced the raw power of God through the blood of Jesus. Who knows if you would be reading this if I had not invoked the blood of Jesus?

We attempted to get out of the vehicle, but the driver noticed that it was dangling off a cliff. In his wisdom, he managed to get out and saw that the two tires were hanging over the cliff while the other two were on the ground. In the nick of time, the blood of Jesus saved us from untimely death; Praise the Lord.

The blood of Jesus works, so use it. No devil or demons can resist the power in the blood of Jesus. In our opening Scripture, we saw that the devil was overcome by the blood of Jesus. If the angels in heaven needed to use the blood to defeat the devil, then you and I have no excuse not to also use it. We must use that blood to achieve victory in our own battles.

PRAYING IN THE SPIRIT

> ***The devil gets confused when you pray in the spirit.***

Years ago I was on a bus in Ghana going to clean a church very early in the morning and I did not have the fare. I didn't want anything to stop me from going to clean the church as a sanctuary keeper, so I asked a passenger sitting by me if he can pay for me, but he refused. I began to speak in tongues, and suddenly the man said to me, "Don't worry I will pay for you." I was not praying in tongues for him to pay for me, I was just communicating with God, and trying not to worry about what the conductor will do when it was time to collect the fare. I had no idea what I was saying, but God heard and answered and I was delivered from shame. That was the first time I experienced the wonder of praying in the Spirit.

> *For if I pray in an unknown tongue, my spirit prayeth, but my understanding is unfruitful.*
> 1 Corinthians 14:14

Praying in the Spirit means it is your own spirit that is praying using your vocal cord. That is why your mind cannot understand what the spirit is saying. Remember man is a spirit, with a soul who lives in a body. This understanding that you are a spirit living in a body will help you to be spirit conscious.

Praying in the Spirit is a strong spiritual weapon.

When you pray in your language, demons hear what you are saying. When you pray in tongues, the devil and his demons cannot understand what you are saying, so they get confused. While they are confused, things are happening in their camp, yokes are broken, and the captives are set free. When you pray in the Spirit, you are saying exactly what moves God to act in line with His will.

> *Praying always with all prayers and supplication in the spirit and watching thereunto with all perseverance and supplication for all saints.*
> Ephesians 6:18

We must learn to pray always in the Spirit. In fact, it will be better if we pray more in the spirit than in our natural language, because it is the Holy Spirit that enables our spirit to pray, and we will pray in accordance with God's will and receive victory over every issue of concern.

THE ANOINTING OIL

The anointing oil can be used in spiritual warfare as led by the Holy Spirit. While you engage in spiritual warfare, the Holy Spirit can reveal something to you that requires anointing. He can ask you to anoint your bed, he can lead you outside your house and show you a specific tree or buried object to anoint, and the plague in your life and family will stop.

> *...and the yoke shall be destroyed*
> *because of the anointing.*
> Isaiah 10:27

There is a testimony of a brother who lost his mother. He couldn't travel to where the mother was, so he anointed the picture of the mother and the mother came back to life. In another instance, a woman and her child were kidnaped by ritual killers. When she was brought to the shrine to be killed, she brought out her anointing oil from her handbag and poured it on the shrine and everything caught fire. The small child she was carrying with her started shouting, "Holy

Ghost fire," and there was confusion in the camp of her captors. There is power in the anointing oil, and it is a powerful spiritual weapon. We need to understand that the wisdom of God is far superior to the wisdom of men. There are many things that seem simple and ineffective in the natural that have nuclear potential in the realm of the spirit.

PRAISE

Praise moves the hand of God. It is a spiritual weapon that cannot fail. When you don't know what to do, try praise. *For God inhabits the praises of his people* (Psalm 22:3). God dwells in praises. When you sing praise to God, you are bringing down His presence and when God comes down, your enemies are crushed. You can't carry the presence of God and suffer defeat or molestation by your enemies. The only way to guarantee God's presence is through praise.

> *Ye shall not need to fight in this battle;*
> *set yourselves, stand ye still, and see*
> *the salvation of the Lord…*
>
> *And when they began to sing and*
> *to praise, the LORD set an ambush*
> *against their enemies (paraphrased)*
> 2 Chronicle 20:17 & 22:

The above text confirms that praise is a powerful weapon in spiritual warfare. You are not required to fight every battle. Begin to praise God and you will see things start to happen. If you lose any member of your family and you don't know what to do, begin to sing and to praise God. I have seen and heard many times the dead coming back to life through praise. If you are sack of your job, instead of crying and asking God why, sing praises. The employer may call you back with a promotion, or a better job offer will come your way. Sometimes we are so emotional that we miss out on certain miracles that would have made us a living testimony. God is looking for men through which He can show Himself strong.

The Scripture says in 2 Chronicles 16:9:

> *For the eyes of the LORD run to and fro throughout the whole earth, to show himself strong on behalf of them whose heart is perfect towards him.*

God wants to prove Himself in your life, and all you need is to position yourself for Him to do so. With praise, you can win every battle in your life. Praise leads to victory. When you become a praise addict, the devil will fear you.

I once read about a former agent of the devil who said that any environment in which God is praised, the demonic agents are uncomfortable. Learn to saturate your environment with praise and worship. Instead of playing secular music which only reminds you of the past or painful moments, why not play worship songs that glorify God?

Some people don't even have praise and worship songs in their cars. There may be times you don't know what to sing. In those instances, you can play praise and worship tape. Whenever I hear a worship song playing, I always feel like going on my knees and worshiping God. That is what such an environment can do. You can even wake up at nights and praise God.

> *And at midnight Paul and Silas prayed, and sang praises unto God: and the prisoners heard them. And suddenly there was a great earthquake, so that the foundations of the prison were shaken: and immediately all the doors were open and everyone's bands were loosed.*
> Acts 16:25-26

When Paul and Silas prayed, nothing happen. When they started to praise, God showed up and everything that held them down began to give way. Paul and Silas did not sing quietly or worry what their neighbors would think. The Bible says **and the prisoners heard them.** When you engage in praise for warfare, don't be too cautious of who will hear or who will complain, and you will see God manifest. Your deliverance will come.

I pray that as you engage in praise as a weapon, everything that binds will give way in Jesus name.

TESTIMONY

Testimony is another spiritual weapon that most Christians don't know much about or understand the power it manifests. The kingdom of darkness wants us to be silent. When you give testimony, it is an announcement to the devil that God is powerful in what He has done, and He will do it again. He will do it for those who hear the testimony, as God is no respecter of persons.

I watched an epic movie and there was a scene where two underworld men met and started casting spells on one another. They began to brag about what they have done to others, and threaten to do the same to each other. What they were doing was giving testimony. Testimonies are powerful and I don't miss an opportunity to share mine in church.

Sometimes a testimony can produce a greater change in someone than preaching. When a man hears someone testify of deliverance and victories, especially if they are experiencing a similar test, they will be encouraged and look forward to their own victory. When you are confronted with any issues of concern, believe that someone has faced that same issue, and God came through for them. If He did it for them, He can do it for you.

> *And they overcame him by the blood of the Lamb and by the word of their testimony;*
> Revelation 12:11:

You can overcome the devil with your testimony. You can overcome any circumstance with your testimony. What God has done for you today is evidence that He can do more tomorrow.

CHAPTER 6

THE BATTLE GROUND

*The battleground of this warfare
is here on the earth.*

As a born again Christian, you are involved in the fight whether you are aware of that reality or not. The day you gave your life to Jesus was the day you entered into battle. Someone may say, "This is making me scared. I think I would be more at peace if I weren't born again." If that is you saying it, then you are wrong because the battle started the day you were conceived in your mother's womb. It gets more intense when you become born again. Those who are not born again are in a worse position because they are the ones that fall victim to the enemy and to what he releases into the world on a regular basis. Because of this, some run to occultic powers for protection, and in so doing complicate their lives and destinies even more.

The following are victims of circumstances:

- ✓ Those who are the first to catch every new sickness or diseases that spring up.
- ✓ The first to die in road or railway accidents.
- ✓ Those on a plane that crashes or disappears.
- ✓ Those who are victims of stray bullets.
- ✓ Those who drown in a river, while others are safely rescued.
- ✓ Those who are accustomed to prisons because of incessant arrests by the police.
- ✓ Those who are victims of collapsed buildings.
- ✓ Those who die of fire or smoke that engulfs a building while they sleep.

More can be added to that list. As long as you are on this earth, you are on the battleground. When you become born again, you become part of the army, and as a soldier, you must fight to defend your territory and your destiny. You must be *Army Strong*®. You must fight to possess the lands God has given to you as an eternal inheritance.

There is a story of a woman who gave birth in a hospital, and there was this midwife who was a witch and part of the midwifery who attended to this woman. According to the witch's confession, as soon as the woman gave birth, she knew through her diabolical means that the baby had a great future. She then collected the baby's destiny through the umbilical cord and sent it to the witchcraft world. This child grew up struggling through life until he met a man of God and his destiny was recovered.

This earth is a constant battleground so there is no escape. The only way to victory is to give your life to Jesus and then fight. The devil was thrown down here, and he came with great anger. Since then he has not taken it easy with anyone. He vowed to destroy man, and he is in the business of doing just that until the end of human time.

I pity those who go to the devil for protection, wealth, and fame. The devil can't protect anyone. His sole desire is to destroy destinies. Show me a man who claims to be under the devil's protection who is not living in fear of every cracking sound at night or flying cockroach. You will hear him screaming and reaching out for his amulet.

Those who have gone to the devil for wealth and fame don't sleep at night because of what they did to get what they wanted. Some even sign a contract to die at a particular age in exchange for fame and when that time comes, they will die mysteriously and their wealth will become meaningless. If people would only come to Jesus, they would live in peace and enjoy abundant lives. All they run after and sell their souls to get, in ignorance, will destroy them.

To be on the safe side, join the Lord's army. Many have lost their lives on the spiritual battlefield, but you will not be one of them. The earth is the battleground and you a soldier who must fight to victory.

THE BATTLEGROUND OF THE MIND

The mind is the number one battleground.

Every action of man begins in the mind as a thought. When the devil wants to afflict a man, he first attacks his mind. The mind is the powerhouse of a man; it is the war front of the forces of good and evil. If you can win the battle in your mind, then you have overcome the battle in the spiritual and physical realms. The state of a man's mind determines the result of every situation in life.

The Scripture says in Proverbs 17:22:

*A merry heart doeth good like a medicine:
but a broken spirit drieth the bones.*

The above Scripture clearly shows that the state of a man's heart plays a significant role in his wellbeing. Some people's minds are so clouded with fear that they can't seem to see the liberty that comes with the gospel of Jesus Christ.

Every act of evil is first conceived in the mind. The assault on our minds every day is the reason we hear and see all the terrible things happening around us. If you want to succeed in life, it will first start with positive thoughts. If you want to be healed and live in sound health, the state of your mind will determine if this will happen or not. The battle in our mind affects our everyday lives. The devil afflicts our minds with negative thoughts; he suggests evil to us with pictures that tend to lure us away from the plan and purpose of God.

In Proverbs 4:23 the Scripture says:

> *Keep thine heart with all diligence;*
> *for out of it are the issues of life.*

Our lives is affected by the state of our hearts (and as a result, our minds), and the Scripture says that we should guard our hearts diligently. Do not give place to the devil and his demons to plant negative thoughts in your mind. The battle against our families, finances, academics, and health can be won if we first win it in our minds. It is the fullness of your mind that you spill out through your utterances. To know the state of a man's mind is to listen to what he says. As a born again Christian soldier, you must guard your heart as you engage in spiritual battle, because it affects your thoughts and mind, which in turn, affects every area of your life.

Do you know that doubt is a battle against your mind to prevent you from exercising faith in God? The forces of wickedness always project doubt (even while you pray) by asking, "Are you sure God can do that for you?" or "Why do you think God is even listening?" If you allow these thoughts to continue by dwelling on them, your faith in God will be overcome by doubt and your prayers will not be answered. When you see failure in your business, know that it is a picture the devil is painting and using to override the original picture of success God painted even before you started that business. If the devil paints a picture that you will not have children, show him the picture that God painted already in Psalm 127:3:

Lo, children are an heritage of the LORD:
and the fruit of the womb is his reward.

God already painted a picture of fruitfulness, so whenever the devil comes with his own picture, quickly show him a copy of God's picture concerning that issue and he will run away. The battle in our minds is an aggressive one, and you must not sleep, but awake and muster all the forces at your disposal to counter the devil's attempts. If you are in a vehicle and the devil starts painting pictures of an accident, remember God's picture in Psalm 91:11:

For he shall give his angels charge over
thee, to keep thee in all thy ways.

If we allow the devil to win our minds, we have lost the battle completely. The state of your mind determines your experiences. Our minds are a battleground and most of the offensives are pictures the devil paints to kill our faith as born again Christians and cause us to doubt what God says. We must fight with positive thoughts and faith in God so we can quench all his fiery darts against our destiny.

As a husband and father, there is a serious battle going on in your mind if you are always angry at your wife and children. When your family hears your voice, do they run and hide as I once did with my stepdad? Does you wife fear talking to you and are your children afraid to be close to you because you are always angry and acting like Lord of all in your house? If so, then there is a serious battle going on. Until you win that battle in your mind, you may lose your beautiful family and those who truly love you.

The devil hates humankind bitterly and tries by every means to destroy man. His number one target is the mind of a man.

Jesus says in Matthew 15:19:

> *For out of the heart proceeds evil thoughts,*
> *murder, adulteries, fornications, theft,*
> *false witness, blasphemies...*

Everything we do is initially thoughts. The actions we take reflect the state our minds. If everyone were to think good thoughts, then we would not have any evil in the world. But the devil is fighting day and night to afflict our minds with negative thoughts, thereby defiling many.

CHAPTER 7

SPIRITUAL ALLIES

In warfare, before you can win, you need allies. Allies are those who help and support you to win a war. There are some battles that without help, you cannot be victorious. While Jesus was praying in the garden of Gethsemane, the Bible records that the angels of God came to strengthen him.

While he was being tempted of the devil after his forty days and nights of fasting, it is recorded that the angels of God came and ministered unto him. We also know about Daniel, who was thrown into the lion's den and God sent His angels, and they closed the mouths of the lions that they could not hurt him.

Angels of God are our spiritual allies.

In the battles of life, we have these spiritual allies whose duties are to help us. There is a path a Christian may never cross in life without angelic intervention. For instance, Joshua would not have succeeded in bringing down the walls of Jericho if not for angelic allies.

> *And it came to pass when Joshua was by Jericho that he lifted up his eyes and looked and behold there stood a man over against him with his sword drawn in his hand, and Joshua went unto him and said unto him, Art thou for us or for our adversary? And he said Nay; but as captain of the host of the Lord am I now come. And Joshua fell on his face to the earth and did worship him and said unto him, what saith my Lord unto his servant?*
> Joshua 5:13-14

We cannot advance or win this spiritual war without angelic allies. Joshua was fighting a battle against Jericho and before he could advance to engage a strong enemy like Jericho, God opened his eyes to see the captain of the angelic armies. What Joshua saw wasn't physical. God had to open his spiritual eyes to see the spiritual allies that had come to help him, and we all know how the battle ended. Jericho was leveled to the ground and everyone in it killed, except Rahab and her family who enlisted on the Lord's side.

Angels are spiritual allies; this knowledge will help you in spiritual warfare. When you stand to pray warfare prayers, any command you issue is being carried out by angels. Angels of God are always on alert to carry out what you say, as long as it is in line with the truth of God's Word.

When you issue a command in line with the Word of God, angels are ready to make sure it is as you said. That is why it is imperative to be full of the Word. As a child of God, you have an angel who follows you everywhere. You may not see him, but he is there and if you don't use him, he will be an untapped resource of strength. Send your angels to work and you may be surprised at the outcome.

I was once owed some money, and every time I went to my debtors, they gave me one excuse after another. One day I went into my prayer time and the Holy Spirit revealed to me that it was not in line with the Word of God that I should be owed, and that I should send my angel. I quickly switched my prayer into warfare prayer. Since I have a guardian angel, I asked the Father to release some angels to me according to Matthew 26:53:

> *Thinkest thou that I cannot now pray to my Father, and he shall presently give me more than twelve legions of angels?*

After praying to the Father, and believing the angels were released according to Mark 11:24:

> *Therefore I say unto you, What things soever ye desire, when ye pray, believe that ye receive them, and ye shall have them.*

I began to release the angels to work for me, giving them the names of those who owed me and how much they owe. To my surprise, the next day, all those who owed me called me, and with apologies, they paid me all the money they owed. Angels can work for you if you send them.

We also know the story of one angel that killed thousands of people in one night in 2 Kings 19:35:

> *And it came to pass that night, that the angel of the LORD went out, and smote in the camp of the Assyrians an hundred fourscore and five thousand: and when they arose early in the morning, behold, they were all dead corpses.*

Angels are very strong, and they can fight for you. What you cannot fight in your own strength, send your angels to do battle for you. The Bible says they excel in strength, so they can do for you what your strength cannot do.

In Egypt, God sent only one angel to kill all the first born of the Egyptians. These spiritual allies are still there for us, and with their help, we can win every battle of life.

CHAPTER 8

AN ENEMY HAS DONE THIS

Anything that is not in line with the truth of God's Word is the enemy at work.

The war that started in heaven continues here on the earth, and this time it's not with the angels but with man. Satan has sworn to destroy man and he is doing that every day by any means. Many fall into the trap of the devil because of spiritual slumber.

The Scriptures in Matthew 13:25 says:

> *But while men slept, his enemy came and sowed tares among the wheat and went his way.*

There are so many things that happen in our lives and we feel it's normal without knowing that there are powerful forces behind those actions and events. There are lots of things we may not do or be involved in, but we are continually drawn to those things by some supernatural forces. If as a born again Christian, any of the things listed later in this chapter describe your life, know that the enemy has sown tares in your life.

Our world is ruled by powerful external forces and these forces are either good or bad. Therefore in this chapter, I will list a few of the things that evil forces, or in this context I will call "an enemy," has done in the lives of many people.

This chapter will open your eyes so that you will know and be able to take steps to stop these evil forces from destroying your life. The Scripture has clearly stated the three-point agenda of our enemy, the devil, who is called the thief in John 10:10:

> *The thief cometh not, but for to **steal**,*
> *and to **kill**, and to **destroy**.*

But there is good news in Proverbs 6:30-31:

> *Men do not despise a thief, if he steals to*
> *satisfy his soul when he is hungry. But if*
> *he is found, he shall restore sevenfold; he*
> *shall give all the substance of his house.*

Thank God that there is restoration for everyone whom the devil has stolen from. The Bible says that when the thief is found, he shall restore sevenfold. You can get a sevenfold restoration from everything the enemy stole from you. If he stole your health, there shall be restoration. If he stole your marriage, finances, business, career, children, etc., there shall be restoration in Jesus name.

The Word of God says if the thief is found, that means there can never be restoration *if the thief is not caught*. You can pass through life without knowing about the thief and so there cannot be any restoration. You must find the thief, and you can do that through the Scripture and this book that you are reading now which will help to reveal any negative events in your life that were caused by the thief. With this knowledge, you have found the thief, and so you begin to demand for restoration.

The Scripture also says in Luke 22:3:

> *Then entered Satan into Judas surnamed Iscariot, being of the number of the twelve.*

If Satan can enter into Judas who was a disciple of Jesus, then he can enter into anyone else to cause confusion in his or her life. In essence, many things that happen are contrary to God's will and are the handiwork of the devil. Satan can enter into anyone and cause them to do what is not right. If we don't acquire the knowledge of the Word of God to know the source, we may conclude that it's natural. Knowledge is power. No more groping in the darkness of ignorance.

If you are of age and not married, an enemy has done this. **Isaiah 34:16**

If you live in a rented apartment for years without being able to buy or build your own house, an enemy has done this. **Isaiah 65:21**

If you have cancer and are about to die, an enemy has done this. **Exodus 23:25-26**

If you are still living with your parent at the age of thirty, an enemy has done this. **Genesis 12:1**

If you bury your children, an enemy has done this. **Isaiah 65:20**

If all you get at the end of the month is what you work for, an enemy has done this. **Proverbs 3:10**

If you have food yet you can't eat, an enemy has done this. **Psalm 128:2**

If all you live by is your weekly or monthly wages, an enemy has done this. **Leviticus 26:10**

If you are married for many years without any child, an enemy has done this. **Psalm 127:3**

If you have an accident and your new car is damaged beyond repair, an enemy has done this. **Psalm 121:8**

If you work and earn wages yet you can't tell exactly where your money goes, an enemy has done this. **Malachi 3:11**

You go to work and your boss fires you without any genuine reason, an enemy has done this. **Exodus 3:21**

You are a beautiful lady and still single at forty, an enemy has done this. **Proverbs 18:22**

If you are involved in an accident that resulted in damage to any part of your body, an enemy has done this. **Psalm 91:11**

If you beg to eat, an enemy has done this. **Psalm 37:25**

If you can't sustain a relationship, an enemy has done this. **Roman 5:5**

If you go to church and sleep while the preacher is preaching, an enemy has done this. **Matthew 13:25**

If you are in a crowd yet you are the only one a stray bullet hits, an enemy has done this. **Psalm 33:18-19**

If you sleep hungry because you don't have anything to eat, an enemy has done this. **Psalm 34:10**

If you slave so that others can get rich, an enemy has done this. **Isaiah 65:22**

If you work while others eat, an enemy has done this. **Isaiah 65:21**

If you commit incest, an enemy has done this. **Leviticus 20:17**

If you are sent to jail but are innocent, an enemy has done this. **Isaiah 42:22**

If you draw a tattoo on your body, an enemy has done this. **Leviticus 19:28**

You are twenty-five years of age and still sag your pants, an enemy has done this. **Romans 1:28**

You propose to many ladies and all their response are, "No," an enemy has done this. **Luke 2:52**

You are driving, suddenly lose control and hit another car and can't understand what just happened, an enemy has done this. **Psalm 91:11**

If you are the chief bridesmaid to all your friends, yet no man has ever proposed to you, an enemy has done this. **Psalm 5:12**

You graduate from college and can't secure a decent job, an enemy has done this. **Genesis 39:4**

You have a PhD yet you never work with it, an enemy has done this. **Psalm 102:13**

Everyone in your line of business is progressing while you still remain on the same spot, an enemy has done this. **Psalm 1:3**

If you are living in debt and borrowing to make ends meet, an enemy has done this. **Deuteronomy 28:12**

The surgeon general warns that smokers are liable to die young yet you still continue to smoke, an enemy has done this. **Hebrew 13:17**

You ask a lady out, she refuses and you decide to rape her, an enemy has done this. **Deuteronomy 22:25-29**

If you sleep with your father's wife, an enemy has done this. **Leviticus 18:8**

In the service of your country, you are trusted with classified information; you decide to betray your country by leaking that information, an enemy has done this. **Proverb 20:7**

You are old and have gray head with no one to love and take care of you, an enemy has done this. **Genesis 24:1**

If your children grow up and refuse to respect you, an enemy has done this. **Proverbs 31:28**

You are an educated beautiful lady with a good career or business yet no man wants to take you out on a date nor marry you, an enemy has done this. **Psalm 102:13**

If you are sick and move from one hospital to another without any cure in sight, an enemy has done this. **Jeremiah 8:22**

If you frequent hospitals because of sickness, an enemy has done this. **Matthew 8:17**

If there is a plague of untimely death in your family, an enemy has done this. **Psalm 91:16**

If no one in your family ever experiences prosperity, an enemy has done this. **3 John 2**

If you are in government and you steal taxpayer's money, an enemy has done this. **Exodus 20:15**

You have people working for you and yet you refuse to pay them when it is due, an enemy has done this. **Deuteronomy 24:14**

If you are involved in insurance fraud, an enemy has done this. **Exodus 20:15**

If you are still a gang or cult member when your mates have denounced it and start going to church, an enemy has done this. **Isaiah 55:6**

If you steal pension funds and because of you, pensioners die untimely deaths, an enemy has done this. **Deuteronomy 24:14**

If you have an important business appointment that will bring you a breakthrough and you miss your flight, an enemy has done this. **Psalm 37:23**

If you are drunk and enter a car to drive, an enemy has done this. **Romans 13:1-7**

If you are a politician and you lie to the people, telling them what you know in your heart that you will never do, an enemy has done this. **Psalm 15:2**

If you are an old man and you are busy dating teenage girls, an enemy has done this. **Proverb 1:7**

If you are involved in child pornography, an enemy has done this. **Romans 1:28**

If you are addicted to pornography, an enemy has done this. **Romans 1;28**

If you are a drug addict, an enemy has done this. **Romans 1:28**

If you have a family yet you refuse to take care of your wife and kids but lavish money on your girlfriend, an enemy has done this. **1 Timothy 5:8**

If instead of you sleeping at nights, you are busy planning the downfall of another man, an enemy has done this. **Proverb 1:11-12**

If whenever you collect your wage, instead of heading home, you decide to visit prostitutes, an enemy has done this. **Roman 1:28**

If you steal money from the church, an enemy has done this. **Exodus 20:15**

If you are a lady, instead of dressing decently, you decide to show every private part of your body in the name of fashion, an enemy has done this. **1Timothy 2:9**

If you are in the habit of beating your spouse, an enemy has done this. **Ephesians 5:33**

If within ten years you have undergone three divorces, an enemy has done this. **Mark 10:9**

While others are sleeping at night, you are busy flying around looking for who to destroy, an enemy has done this. **Exodus 22:18**

If you refuse Jesus and chose the devil, an enemy has done this. **John 3:16**

If in the name of getting rich quick, you sell your soul to the devil, an enemy has done this. **Proverb 10:22**

You are sick, yet doctors can't find any sickness in you during a test, an enemy has done this. **Isaiah 53:5**

If you are in the habit of gambling and you have gambled all your life savings and now you don't have anything to show for all your efforts and years of service, an enemy has done this. **Proverb 17:25**

If you see yourself flying at night while asleep, an enemy has done this. **Ezekiel 13:18-20**

You belong to a church and yet you don't pay your tithe, an enemy has done this. **Malachi 3:10**

If you are in the habit of sleeping with all the ladies in your church, an enemy has done this**. 1 Thessalonians 4:3**

If you keep seeing dead relatives in your dreams at night, an enemy has done this. **Mark 12:27**

From the above list, we can see some of the things the enemy has done in the lives of people. But we have also seen related Scriptures to support that these things are contrary to God's plan and purpose for our lives. You must do something and know that it is a fight you must win.

CHAPTER 9

WHY YOU MUST NOT LOSE THE FIGHT

You cannot afford to lose this fight. To lose this fight is very dangerous. During the days of the Roman Empire, two prisoners would be brought into the arena, given swords and instructed to fight to the death. Only one prisoner will be left standing. That is the same scenario we face today: To live we must fight.

> *...through the greatness of thy power shall thine enemies submit themselves unto thee.*
> Psalm 66:3

For the enemy to submit, you must exercise your authority as a victor. If you don't win, they won't submit. Life cannot give you more than what you have put into it. For things to go the way you want, you must put your enemies under control. You cannot afford to be casual about life. You need to be mindful that your enemy the devil and his host of demons are against you, so to survive you must win the war; you must stay alert and fight. Do not give in or make excuses. Either you fight to win or the enemy will deal severely with you.

If you are losing the battle, it will make you a beggar while others are shining. You will be prone to sickness, poverty, harassment and affliction. For you to enjoy life to the fullest, you must win the war against the forces of darkness that come against you.

Failure is painful.

Ask a student who failed an exam how they felt. You will understand that failure is painful and shameful. You cannot afford to lose because it will be very painful and shameful to do so, and the consequences will be unbearable. Everyone wants success and that comes with a cost. You must pay the price to succeed in your war against the army of darkness. The number one source of success is the Bible.

In 2 Timothy 2:15 the Scripture says:

> *Study to shew thyself approved unto God, a workman that needeth not to be ashamed, rightly dividing the word of truth.*

You must study the Bible to be free from shame and to be able to succeed. Let the Word of God be your companion and faithful friend and it will not fail you. Meditate daily on the Word of God and you will build enough ammunition to fight the devil any day, any time.

CHAPTER 10

STRATEGIC SPIRITUAL WARFARE

Fighting a spiritual battle requires knowledge and this knowledge is embedded in the Word of God. Without knowledge, you cannot succeed.

Every day your enemy the devil formulates new strategies against you. Therefore, you must be updated and upgraded to conquer him and his cohorts. The knowledge of their *modus operandi* is vital in this warfare.

Witches have a way of getting to people these days, especially children. They can initiate or afflict through a simple gift of candy, etc. To secure your children, anoint them before they go to school, give them communion and make it mandatory. Start early in their lives so they get used to it, teach them how to plead the blood of Jesus.

Every responsible and supposedly good child reflects the kind of home they come from. If you see a child sagging his pants, piercing and or drawing tattoos all over his body, know for sure that the child may not be from a responsible home. As a parent, you must learn to guide your children and put them on the right track. Don't expose them to the devil's assaults saying "They will learn as they grow." You may not be able to rescue them.

As a little boy, my mother taught me how to say, "I cover myself with the blood of Jesus. I plead the blood of Jesus over my life." This declaration has helped me a lot. I would not be alive today if I did not constantly profess my insurance policy, which is the blood of Jesus. There were times I was acutely afflicted, but I kept saying those words and the affliction would go.

The night season is the time that many things happen spiritually. Most of the things that happen during the day are the results of what happens during the night. Witches can barbecue someone, eat that person and clean their mouth while that individual is still alive physically, but dead spiritually. Someone who appears to be healthy can just die suddenly. What we may not know is that person was already dead. They may have been killed spiritually and were awaiting someone who would take the blame for the physical death. No Christian should take this information lightly because they are real. Many things are going on in life that we are not aware of. We need knowledge.

A man was praying with his family one early morning when they heard a loud bang on their roof. They rushed out to see what it was. There was a naked old woman crawling and trying to hide herself. They began to question her, threatening to hit her if she didn't respond. When she saw the crowd and the day breaking, she said she was on her way back from a meeting. As she was flying across their roof, a strong force like a magnet pulled her down and she fell off the roof and rolled to the ground.

This earth is very deep. While you are in your house at night, there are people who don't sleep who are busy flying around perpetrating wickedness. If that man had not been praying with his family, that witch would have escaped. That family's battle-ready life caused that agent of the devil to crashland, and people's destinies were delivered.

Strategic spiritual warfare is not for pastors or prayer warriors only. It is for every believer. You don't know who your neighbor is, or who the colleague in your office truly is, or your children's school teachers. You need to be battle-ready always. Not everyone you see or know in church is a normal human being. Witches come to church also. The people you love and trust and think of as holy brothers or sisters may not be who you think they are. You rub shoulders every Sunday in church with agents of the devil, who may have just got back from a meeting in the marine world the night before. Not everyone on the streets is normal, some are highly demonized.

I read a story of a school teacher who collected children's academic destinies, and kept them in the spirit world. Suddenly these children who were brilliant become very dull in school and their grades deteriorated. One day while a sister was praying, she saw their teacher sitting on the moon in an occultic posture. She knew then that the teacher wasn't ordinary, so this sister went and confronted her in the school. She told the teacher to release the children or she would die. The teacher apologized and said "I didn't know you knew." Those children were released and their intellect restored.

The Bible says in Psalm 74:20:

> *For the dark places of the earth are*
> *full of the habitations of cruelty.*

The devil does not love you and will never do. He is fighting every second to bring you down. He enters family homes to destroy marriages, and this is his primary point of attack because when homes are destroyed, the nation will be destroyed and the world will not be a better place. He is out to spoil everything God has made. He is busy matching the wrong people in marriage. He causes accidenst on land, sea, and in the air every day. Just turn on your television and you will see the devil at work.

God is never the source of evil. He is a good God. He wants you to accept His Son as the only way to escape the wickedness of the devil. If a train derails with many casualties, it is not the fault of the train driver. There are powers beyond what we see, so blaming the driver is pointless. Our war is not against the physical. We are so accustomed to the physical aspects of life that we forget that this world is ruled by the spiritual world. An airplane loaded with passengers may disappear without a trace. This should not be attributed to physical faults. Another airplane may purposely be crashed by a co-pilot. It is not suicide. These things are not normal.

We talk of aliens every day, yet we don't ask where they come from. God created all things in this world. God did not create separate beings and put them on another planet.

We just need to observe how teenagers are behaving these days to see that clearly there is something out to destroy us. The battle is very intense and we are at the front of the war. We cannot afford to lag behind. There are witches in church every Sunday. They easily become very active members, and sometimes they are people you may love and trust. If God were to open your eyes, you would be consumed with fear at what you would see.

Many people believe that when we give our lives to Jesus the journey will be very smooth, but life is warfare and not a playfare.

Jesus told his disciples in Mark 11:23:

> *For verily I say unto you, that whosoever shall say unto this **mountain**, be thou removed, and be thou cast into the sea...*

The mountain is there, but you must speak to it. It is up to you to do something about your situations or else nothing can be done. If you notice that you keep failing your exam, then that is a battle you must wake up and fight to win. It is not a normal fight until you pass the exam with flying colors.

If your wife starts spending too much time on social media rather than reading the Bible, that is an attack from the camp of the enemy. She is not the cause, but the enemy will use that to ruin your home. Don't keep silent and accept that as normal behaviour or she will change. Fight back with all the weapons at your disposal.

I have an uncle who was very wealthy. He was the star in the family, and every road led to his house. If you were hungry or needed money for school, he was the one to go to. When you got there, all your problems were solved. Suddenly everything shattered. He lost his contracts, and his job. He closed his business and started selling his cars and possessions. Food became scarce and we all wondered why. He went from one prayer house to another but no solution.

One day, while his wife was bathing his son, she noticed a wound on the boy and asked how he got it. The boy said it was grandma. She asked, "How did my husband's mother give you this wound?" His reply was that grandma always came at midnight to call him out to the witchcraft world, and put him on her back and flew out for meeting. The boy began to narrate how he drove his father's car at night and in the morning the engine will knock. He told the mother that he was the reason why his father lost everything.

This incident emphasizes that we are not fighting physical enemies. The boy was initiated into witchcraft by his grandmother, and his mission was to destroy the father. Until today, my uncle has not recovered from the damage the boy did. Don't give place to the devil. Every born again Christian needs to know that this warfare is spiritual, so you must keep your eyes open. Find out who your children are friends with, where they go, and what they do. It is an error to allow a child do all that he or she wants to do, believing that he or she will learn as he or she grow.

Your children are given to you to take care of. What you don't take care of is bound to decay. A responsible child cannot sag his pant and you allow him walk out of your house. That will never show that he is coming out of a responsible home. Your daughter should not come home one day with tattoos and piercings and you smile and welcome her. You would be in agreement to help destroy the destiny of that child. It is your God-given responsibility to take care of your children. Learn to talk with your children. They are the future. Ask them questions when they come from school. Ask how their day was and what they did. Talk with them, you never know what you may find out, and with God's wisdom at work in your life you will help direct them. The best gift you can give your children is to take them to church, point them to Jesus, and they will grow to make you proud.

You may be in a situation where you see others being promoted in their jobs, and you are not. As a Christian, you are the one that should be promoted before anyone else.

You may be married and not have children and you keep quiet for many years when you know that is not the plan of God for you. The Hebrew women were so fruitful that the Bible records that before the midwives came in, the children were already born. They were so fruitful that Pharaoh was afraid the Egyptians would be outnumbered. (Exodus 1:1-22)

When you give your life to Jesus, you automatically become adopted into the family of God, and are a daughter of Abraham through that adoption, and fruitfulness runs in the family so you have no business being barren.

You should not be applying for jobs and getting continually rejected. It should not happen to you.

Sickness and diseases are not your portions because Jesus, your senior brother, paid the price for your total health. The devil is making you sick, so you must fight back to get your freedom. Jesus died and paid the price for you to live a glorious and dignified life. Anything less than that is an attack from the enemy and you must fight to conquer.

Strategic spiritual warfare must be the lifestyle of every believer. There is a war going on and your enemy is fighting, whether you are aware or not. We often think that spiritual warfare is exclusive and reserved for some specific people or church denomination. I have heard some people say if you want to fight the devil go to a particular church. You don't have to go to a particular church to fight your enemy. You are already fighting as a born again believer. All you need is knowledge so you can fight and win.

If you consistently run after pastors to pray for you every time there is an issue, you are acting immature. It is not wrong to go to a pastor for prayer, but it should not be your attitude every time you are confronted with challenges. Learn to take responsibility and use what you have. The pastors have the same authority and faith that you have. The only difference is, they have learnt to use it and you haven't.

Strategic spiritual warfare requires adequate intake of the Word of God.

> *This book of the law shall not depart out of*
> *thy mouth; but thou shall meditate therein*
> *day and night, that thou mayest observe to*
> *do according to all that is written therein:*
> *for then thou shall make thy way prosperous,*
> *and then thou shall have good success.*
> Joshua 1:8

Success in spiritual warfare requires you to study the Scriptures. The Word you study today might just be the Word you need when fighting a particular battle tomorrow. Whatever you study is never lost, but is kept within you. When an occasion demands, the Holy Spirit goes into your spirit and brings it out; because the Word is already there. What you don't store can't come out.

One day, I was faced with a situation, and while talking to God in prayer, I suddenly saw a Scripture flash through my mind from Isaiah 41:17-18:

> *When the poor and the needy seek water, and there is none, and their tongue faileth for thirst, I the God of Israel will not forsake them. I will open rivers in high places, and fountains in the midst of the valleys: I will make the wilderness a pool of water, and the dry land springs of water.*

I was comforted by those words. I knew I had read them, but couldn't place where it was in the Bible. I went in search of them and found them. If I did not study the Bible, the Holy Spirit would not have had anything to comfort me with at that moment.

Word intake is vital, like loading a bullet into a gun. When you come under attack, all you need to do is pull the trigger and fire. Many of us have been firing an empty gun, and that is why there has been no result.

Why should you be sleeping at night when spirits are inflicting you? If you keep quiet, you don't know who you are. Maybe that is why they are messing with you.

Some time ago, I was asleep when I realized that someone was sitting on my bed. It was a dark figure. I felt heavy and could not turn. I was pressed. I tried to say the blood of Jesus, and my mouth was heavy. I began to get angry in the spirit because I knew what was going on. I struggled until I jumped up from the bed. Instead of pleading the blood of Jesus as usual, I remembered the Scripture that says:

> *When thou liest down, thou shall not*
> *be afraid: yea, thou shall lie down,*
> *and thy sleep shall be sweet*
> Proverbs 3:24

Another Scripture says in Psalm 127:2:

> *It is in vain for you to rise up early, to sit*
> *up late, to eat the bread of sorrows:*
> ***for so he giveth his beloved sleep.***

I gathered all these Scriptures together and begin to declare it aloud, "Night is for sleep. God gives his beloveth sleep and am his beloveth. He says I shall lay down and sleep and my sleep shall be sweet, and nothing shall make me afraid. It is only the counsel of the Lord that shall stand in my life; therefore, anyone that say I shall not sleep this night shall face the judgment of God. I call down fire to destroy anything that is contrary to the plan and purpose of God in my life. Let God arise, let His enemies be scattered, let them that hate Him flee. I decree destruction upon any dark forces that are out against me this night." I began to command the angels of God to arrest any foul spirit at work around me. I was outraged in the spirit because like Paul said in Ephesian 5:3:

> *Let it not be once named among*
> *you, as becometh saints*

How can I be pressed by witches and wizards as a child of God!? That was the end of that affliction. I slept like a baby, and I have been sleeping like that since. If you keep silent, evil spirits will mess you up because a closed mouth is a closed destiny. If you know your authority and right and decide to put on your armour and fight back, then life will be sweet.

The mishaps we see or hear every day are caused by wicked forces. Don't embark on a journey without first taking the offensive to the gates of your enemy.

As a young boy, before traveling, I would pray "As I travel, I shall consume the road. The road shall not consume me. I plead the blood of Jesus over the road that I will take." I don't know how the prayer came, but I prayed it. I love to travel, so every journey must be pleasant and it has always been. If you are preparing to travel, listen to your spirit. Don't wake up one day and decide to travel. I am in the habit of not telling people that I am traveling. If my spirit is not comfortable with the journey, I don't go. I must be free in the spirit and be joyful when traveling. Any heaviness in my spirit spells danger.

Search your life, and note things that keep recurring. For instance, experiencing accidents at the same spot every year; falling sick at a particular month every year; having a miscarriage when a particular family member or friend visits or is informed that you are pregnant;

or having a fever every time you go for a job interview or promotional exam. These are all attacks from the enemy and you should not take them lightly, but instead fight back.

Joshua was fighting a battle and it seemed that the day would end and they would lose the fight. He did something no man had ever done, and spoke to the sun to stand still:

> *Then spake Joshua to the Lord in the day when the Lord delivered up the Amorites before the children of Israel, Sun stand thou still upon Gibeon and thou moon in the valley of Ajalon. And the sun stood still and the moon stayed until the people had avenged themselves upon their enemies. Is not this written in the book of Jasher? So the sun stood still in the midst of heaven and hasted not to go down about a whole day. And there was no day like that before it or after it, that the Lord hearkened unto the voice of man, for the Lord fought for Israel.*
> Joshua 10:12-14

In spiritual warfare, all you need is a command. Joshua did not have a discussion with the sun and the moon, but instead he issued a command and the ordinance obeyed him.

The devil has no respect for long grammar or eloquent speech, but he listens to a command and obeys. The above Scripture shows that Joshua did not plead with the situation, he didn't ask God to come and help him. The challenge at that moment was the impending darkness which would hinder him from the breakthrough he needed. He issued a command and the command was specific: *Sun stand thou still* and the sun stood still because the ordinances of heaven have ears.

Very often we pray, but we don't tell the situation what we want. We must learn to be specific and say what we want. If we do, we will get the results that we desire.

When there was darkness on the formless earth and God decided to recreate it, He didn't negotiate with it, all He did was issue a command in Genesis 1:3:

> *...let there be light: and there was light.*

God did not explain to the darkness or reasoned with it, all He did was say what He wanted and He got the results. Your command must be accompanied by faith, for without faith it is impossible to please God (Hebrew 11:6). Joshua was able to move God to act because he had absolute trust in God, and that pleased God.

Never issue a command and doubt or wonder how it is going to happen. Simply believe that what you command will manifest. Jesus said, "*If you have faith as a grain of mustard seed you shall say unto any mountain to move and they will obey you."* (Luke 17:6)

You must be bold when engaging in spiritual warfare. I had a stepfather who was involved in the occult. One day he had a meeting at midnight with the occultic people who came into the house spiritually. My mother started praying and while she was praying, we were hearing a group of men chanting in the living room. My mother could not wait for them to finish, so she opened the door. A strong breeze from the living room blew away everything in the room and almost carried away my mom, but she shouted "Jesus," and all those men disappeared. My stepdad was very upset. I was a little boy then, but I admired my mother's boldness because we were all afraid, but she was not. If my mum was afraid, I don't think she would have survived that season in her life.

Boldness in warfare is necessary because no soldier enters a war in fear or if he does, he will be an easy target.

When God first spoke to Joshua, He told him three times to be bold and of good courage. Joshua 1:6, 7, 9:

> *Be strong and of a good courage…*
> *Only be thou strong and very courageous…*
> *Have not I commanded thee? Be strong*
> *and of a good courage; be not afraid,*
> *neither be thou dismayed…*

You need boldness to command witches and wizards to die. You need boldness to enter your father's secret room and destroy all satanic deposits that have been afflicting you and your family. You need boldness to confront that occultic husband of yours and draw the line, like my mother did, bringing an end to his operations in your family.

Strategic spiritual warfare is not for lazy Christians but for those who are determined to take their destinies into their own hands. God has freely given us all things that pertain to live and godliness, but we must fight to experience them.

Those prayers you pray while lying on your couch or comfortable bed are not warfare prayers. Take some days to fast and outline Scriptures that you will use. A soldier who is gearing up for war will take the time to select his weapons and get prepared before entering the war. There are giants in every man's way to his Canaan, so you must first kill the giants before you can enter your promised land.

Every time God promises you something, the devil and his agents are aware of those promises and they will do everything possible to make sure you don't experience them. You have the responsibility to take matters into your hands so that you can enjoy God's avowed blessings.

The world is coming to an end, wickedness is on the increase, and your awareness of the attack from the enemy will help you to be on alert, to be prepared and to fight back.

CHAPTER 11

VICTORY

Victory is sweet.

There is nothing like the feeling of a job well done. There is nothing like the sound of victory. At the end of every war, the winning side always has a celebration in their camp, while those who lose will either be weeping or remain quiet with their head bowed down.

When you overcome the devil, you will be joyful and celebrate.

> *For whatsoever is born of God overcometh the world: and this is the victory that overcometh the world even our faith. Who is he that overcometh the world, but he that believeth that Jesus is the Son of God?*
> 1 John 5:4

As a born again child of God, you, by divine inheritance, have overcome the devil and his agents. The Bible says that when you are born again that your victory is sure, so believing in Jesus has guaranteed your victory. When you know that God has granted you victory in the battles of life, it will help you to be positioned to experience it.

When Jesus rose from the dead, he said:

> *...all power is given unto me...*
> Matthew 28:18

Your enemy is a toothless dog, and he is just barking. Do not be afraid to attack and destroy him. In spiritual warfare, we are destined to win.

Faith is a major factor in spiritual warfare. Faith helps you to quench all the arrows the enemy will throw at you. Without faith, you cannot succeed in warfare. You must take to yourself the shield of faith. This will protect you and will move God on your behalf. The subject of faith in strategic spiritual warfare cannot be overemphasized because it is the believer's life wire. It is the force of our existence. When you engage faith in your fight, the battle is won.

God will never move until your faith is in place. For you to get God to commit to your affairs, you must have absolute trust in him. When you trust Him, your victory is sure.

Note from the Publisher

Are you a first time author?

Not sure how to proceed to get your book published?
Want to keep all your rights and all your royalties?
Want it to look as good as a Top 10 publisher?
Need help with editing, layout, cover design?
Want it out there selling in 90 days or less?

Visit our website for some exciting new options!

www.chalfant-eckert-publishing.com

If you have been blessed, impacted or given your life to Jesus through reading this book, please let me know through the following means:

victoransor@gmail.com
Twitter: @victoransor
Facebook: Victor Ansor

God Bless You.

www.ingramcontent.com/pod-product-compliance
Lightning Source LLC
Chambersburg PA
CBHW030332080526
44584CB00012B/820